The Magic School Bus

PRESENTS

Planet Earth

Scholastic Inc.

Previous page: A canyon in Zion National Park, Utah

Photos ©: Alamy Images/Michele Falzone: 16 background, 17; Corbis Images: 28 top left (George Steinmetz), 31 left (Jenny E. Ross), 28 bottom left (Joe Carini/Design Pics), 21 (Sandro Vannini); Getty Images: 28 bottom right (Alexey Avdeev), 14 bottom (Can Balcioglu), 4 top left (Christian Kober), cover background (Christophe Lehenaff), 29 top left (Eco/UIG), 28 top right (Erik Sampers), 26 bottom (G. Brad Lewis), 6 background, 7 (Ilia Shalamaev www.focuswildlife.com), 3 center, 16 top left (Jeff Foott/Discovery Channel Images), 23 bottom left (Ken Lucas/Visuals Unlimited), 3 top, 12 (Ken Welsh), 10 (Kevin Schafer), 13 bottom (Mint Images - Frans Lanting), 14 top (PhotoStock-Israel), 3 bottom, 26 background, 27 (Richard A Cooke III), 24 top left (Stephen Alvarez/National Geographic Creative), 26 top (Ulet Ifansasti), 6 top left (Visuals Unlimited, Inc./Stephen Ingram); iStockphoto: 1 (LifeJourneys), 4 background, 5 (miljko); National Geographic Creative: 20 left (Greg Dale), 20 bottom right (Jason Edwards), 29 bottom left (Peter Carsten); Nature Picture Library: 8 right (Alex Mustard), 29 bottom right (Hanne & Jens Eriksen), 20 top right (Juan Carlos Munoz), top right (Leo & Mandy Dickinson), 13 top (Orsolya Haarberg), 24 background, 25 (Steven David Miller); Science Source: 11 bottom (Adrienne Hart-Davis/Photo Researchers, Inc.), 19 left (Alfred Pasieka), 22 (Chris Knapton/Photo Researchers), 9 (David Parker), 18 (Javier Trueba/MSF), 11 left, 23 top left (Joel Arem), 15 (John Shaw), 31 right (Jon Wilson), 19 center (Joyce Photographics), 19 right, 23 right (Photo Researchers), 30 (Stephen J. Krasemann); Shutterstock, Inc./Loskutnikov: cover; Superstock, Inc./Ragnar Th. Sigurdsson/age fotostock: 8 left.

ISBN 978-0-545-68012-7

Produced by Potomac Global Media, LLC

All text, illustrations, and compilation © 2014 Scholastic Inc.
Based on The Magic School Bus series © Joanna Cole and Bruce Degen
Text by Tom Jackson Illustrations by Carolyn Bracken
Consultants: Rainer Newberry, Geology Professor, University of Alaska; Dr. Douglas Palmer, science writer and lecturer, Institute of Continuing Education, Cambridge University, England; and Peter Rinkleff, Ph.D., geoscience and volcanology

Published by Scholastic Inc., 557 Broadway, New York, NY 10012.

12 11 10 9 8 7 6 5 4 3 2   14 15 16 17 18 19/0

Cover design by Paul Banks
Interior design by Carol Farrar Norton
Photo research by Sharon Southren

Printed in the U.S.A.   40
First printing, July 2014

Contents

p. 12

p. 16

p. 26

Up High

Ms. Frizzle told our class, "Today we're going up as high as we can go." At 29,035 feet (8,850 meters) high, Mount Everest is the highest place on planet Earth. Once we reached the top, we learned how the Earth got to be so mountainous.

The climb to the top of Mount Everest takes several days and is very dangerous. Climbers sleep in tents on the way up.

The first people to climb to the top of Everest were Edmund Hillary and Tenzing Norgay in 1953.

Top of the world
The wind at Everest's summit travels at 110 miles (180 kilometers) per hour. Temperatures can reach 31 degrees below zero Fahrenheit (minus 35 degrees Celsius).

Mountain range
Everest is part of a mountain range called the Himalayas. It lies between Nepal and Tibet in Asia.

Shifting plates!

How mountains form
by Carlos

The Earth's surface, or crust, is made up of huge slabs of rock called plates. The plates move around very slowly. Sometimes one plate collides with another, causing a thick bulge to form. This bulge is a mountain range.

plate

mountain range

When plates collide

plate

Frizzle Fact
The rocks at the top of Mount Everest have tiny seashell fossils in them. The shells show that the rocks used to be underwater 450 million years ago.

Down Low

The Dead Sea in Israel and Jordan is the lowest place on Earth. At its deepest, the sea is 2,590 feet (790 meters) below sea level. Even its shores are as low as 1,300 feet (400 meters) below sea level in places. The Dead Sea is part of the Jordan Rift Valley. A rift is a huge crack in the surface of the Earth.

The Dead Sea is eight times saltier than ocean water.

Death Valley is the lowest place on dry land in the United States. It is also the hottest place in North America.

Frizzle Fact

In 100 million years, Death Valley will have joined the ocean, making the state of California a peninsula.

It's cracking up!

Moving apart
by Wanda

A rift is a crack that forms between two of the plates that make up Earth's crust. As two plates move away from each other, the crack between them gets wider and deeper. Over time, rifts like the East Africa Rift Valley — a crack in the African Plate — will grow so big that they reach the ocean, and water will flood in.

plate

plate

When plates separate

Easy to float
High levels of salt make the water more dense. This means swimmers can float with barely any effort.

No plants or creatures can live in such salty water.

I like salt on my fries!

Salt crystals
Salt is one of more than 30 types of minerals found in the water. The minerals form crystals along the shoreline.

An Earthquake Fault

Any place where rocks break and slide past each other is called a fault. Really big zones of faults are caused by Earth's plates moving past one another. These movements can create different rock formations, such as rifts and ridges. They may even cause earthquakes to happen.

Many rifts lie underwater, including the Silfra Rift in Thingvallavatn Lake, in Iceland.

This is Reykjanes Ridge in Iceland. Ridges are long, narrow, raised lines or chains of hills.

The San Andreas Fault is more than 800 miles (1,280 km) long.

The plates are moving by up to 1.5 inches (3.8 centimeters) a year.

Gives me the shakes!

How earthquakes happen
by Phoebe

Earthquakes are common in faults where two plates are moving in opposite directions to each other. Sometimes they get stuck so that neither plate can move. As stress builds up, the plates crack and move in sudden jolts. The jolts make the rocks in the area shake for several seconds.

plate

plate

The San Andreas Fault runs along the coast of California, where the North American plate meets the Pacific plate.

Studying the Ground

This giant rock was a tube of magma (melted rock) that fed a volcano. The volcano and the rocks surrounding this "tube" have crumbled away.

That's Ship Rock in New Mexico.

It has become exposed through millions of years of erosion.

No one can go deep enough inside the Earth to see what it looks like. By studying rock formations, earthquakes, and volcanoes above the surface, scientists can learn about what is happening deep inside the planet.

Let's get deep!

What's inside Earth?
by Ralphie

Planet Earth is made up of layers. The outer layer, where we live, is called the Earth's crust. It is made from hard rocks. The crust sits on top of a layer of denser rock (called the mantle) like a tangerine peel enclosing a tangerine. The center of the planet is the core. The outer core is a blob of hot liquid iron. The inner core is a spinning ball of solid iron.

mantle — outer core
inner core
crust

The ball of iron at the center of the Earth is rotating. This motion makes the planet magnetic. Some iron-rich rocks behave like magnets, too.

Travelers and navigators use magnetic compasses to help them find north.

Frizzle Fact

The deepest hole ever drilled is in Russia. It is just over 7.5 miles (12 kilometers) deep. That far down, the rock is so hot the drill began to melt.

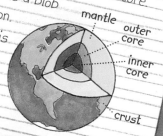

The Power of Water

Angel Falls in Venezuela is three times taller than the Eiffel Tower.

A waterfall forms where a river wears away the softer rock in the riverbed, while leaving a tall cliff of harder rock still standing.

Planet Earth is the only place in the solar system that has water on its surface. Most of Earth's crust is under the sea. On land, falling rain and rivers wear away the rocks, turning them to sand and dust. Over millions of years, rivers will even wear away the tallest mountains until they are flat.

Rivers cut valleys and canyons through rocks, washing the fragments of sand out to sea.

Wear and tear!

Glaciers

Snowy source
The ice in a glacier comes from mountain snow that builds up over many centuries.

Flowing ice
Glaciers are rivers of flowing ice. They move downhill very slowly, grinding away at the rocks underneath.

That is very cool!

From ice to water
Glacial ice melts to form a lake. Some of the world's largest rivers start at these lakes.

Weathering and erosion
by Dorothy Ann

Rocks change and get broken into smaller and smaller lumps by a natural process called weathering. Erosion happens when these pieces of rock are carried away. These are some of the things that happen:
• Water that is full of sand and grit grinds away at rock like sandpaper.
• Water that freezes inside a crack swells, making the crack wider.
• Chemicals in rainwater attack the rock, making it weak and crumbly.

Types of Rocks

There are three main types of rocks. Igneous rocks form when hot lava and magma cool down and solidify. Sedimentary rocks are made from rock fragments that build up in layers. Each layer becomes compressed over many centuries until it hardens. Metamorphic rocks are rocks that were changed from one kind to another by heat and pressure.

Basalt
This igneous rock started as lava from a volcano. As it cooled, the rock cracked into sections, eventually forming columns.

Limestone
This sedimentary rock is made from shells of dead sea animals. The shells sank to the bottom of the sea. The layers of shells were compressed over time and eventually became rock.

Frizzle Fact

Egypt's Great Pyramid is the largest stone building on Earth. It is made of more than two million limestone blocks.

Using rocks

by Wanda

Rocks have a lot of uses. Blocks of some rocks are hard and stiff and good for making the walls of buildings. Softer ones, such as marble, can be carved into shapes. Many of the world's greatest statues are made from marble. Slate is a type of rock that splits into flat sheets. It is used to make tiles for roofs and floors. Tiny specks of limestone are even fed to chickens. The chemicals in the rock help the birds make strong eggshells.

Building blocks!

Marble

This metamorphic rock formed when limestone was heated and compressed deep underground. Shell fragments became small, shiny crystals.

Wow! The steady action of the waves has worn the marble smooth over time.

The Grand Canyon

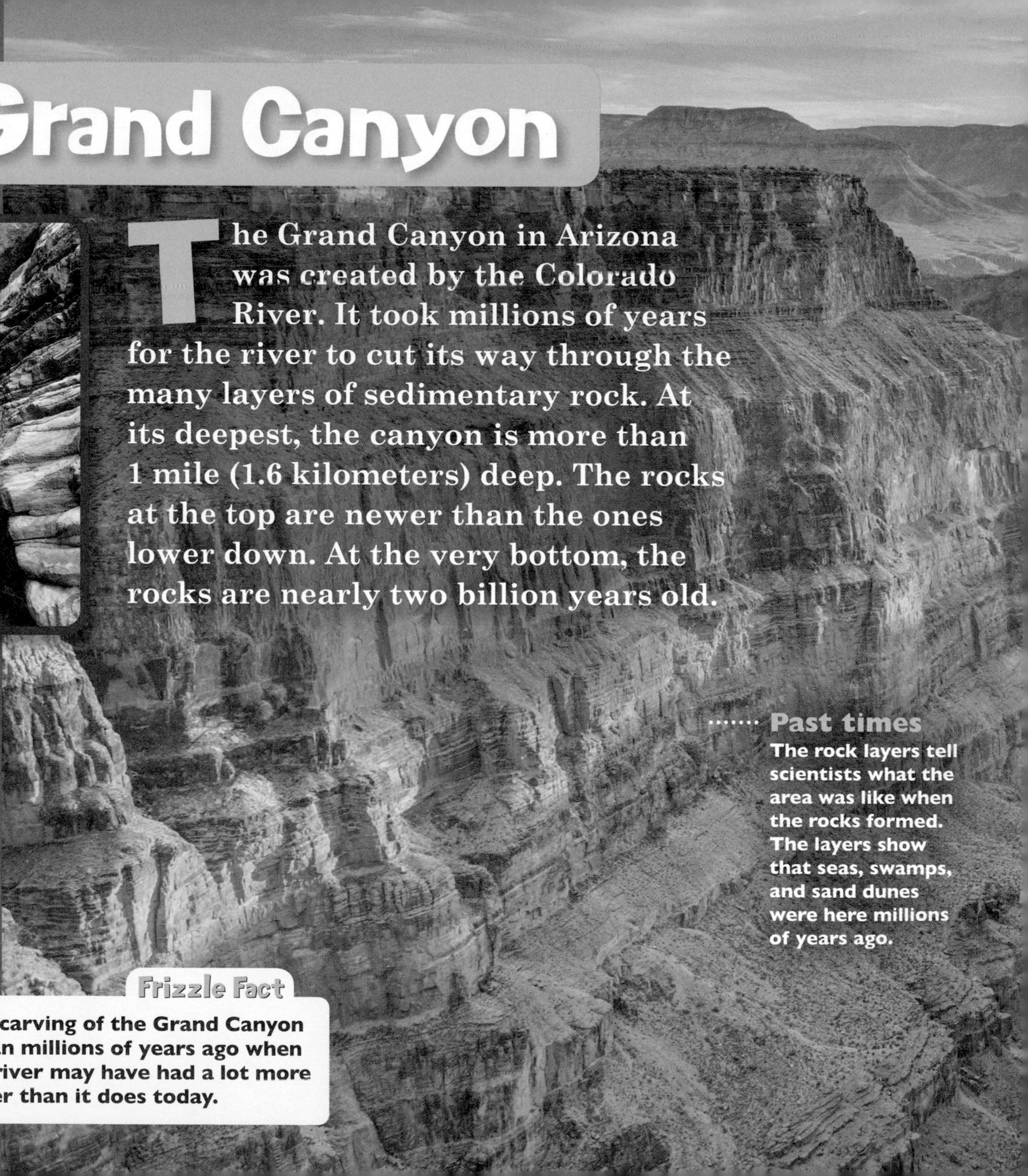

The Grand Canyon in Arizona was created by the Colorado River. It took millions of years for the river to cut its way through the many layers of sedimentary rock. At its deepest, the canyon is more than 1 mile (1.6 kilometers) deep. The rocks at the top are newer than the ones lower down. At the very bottom, the rocks are nearly two billion years old.

The Grand Canyon is in a desert. Any rain that falls trickles into creeks that spill into the canyon as waterfalls.

Past times

The rock layers tell scientists what the area was like when the rocks formed. The layers show that seas, swamps, and sand dunes were here millions of years ago.

Frizzle Fact

The carving of the Grand Canyon began millions of years ago when the river may have had a lot more water than it does today.

Four million people visit the Grand Canyon every year.

It's wearing away!

Red river
The name Colorado means "red-colored" in Spanish. The river water is red from all the clay and silt in it.

How the Grand Canyon formed
by Tim

The Colorado River starts far away in the Rocky Mountains. It carries water from melting snow all the way to the sea in the Gulf of California. That's 862 miles (1,388 kilometers). Around 60 million years ago the central part of Arizona was pushed up into mountains. The river wore away at the rocks as they rose higher, creating the canyon.

17

Minerals and Crystals

These crystals are 1,000 feet (300 meters) belowground.

The biggest crystal in this cave is 50 feet (15 meters) long. That's as long as a big-rig trailer.

Giant crystals
These pillars of gypsum in the Cave of Crystals in Naica, Mexico, are the largest crystals ever found.

Rocks are made of ingredients called minerals. There are around 0,000 different minerals found on Earth, and every rock is made from a different set of them. Many minerals exist as crystals. A close-up look at a rock often reveals that it is made from tiny crystals locked together.

What are minerals used for?
by Ralphie

Here are some common uses of the minerals found in rocks:
- Tiny flecks of feldspar worn off rocks become clay, which is used to make china and pottery.
- Mica is added to paints and makeup to make them shiny.
- Gypsum is used to make cement.
- Quartz crystals are the main minerals in sand.
- Perhaps the most familiar mineral of all is the salt — or sodium chloride — we sprinkle on our food.

Under the microscope

Slice of rock
Rock is cut into thin slices so the different crystals can be examined more closely.

Shining lights
Experts look at rocks under special lights. The colors of the crystals show which minerals they are made of.

Granite
Rocks that form by cooling slowly deep underground have large crystals that are easy to see. The colored flecks in granite are crystals.

Geode
A hole forms inside some rocks as they become solid. The space is often filled with beautiful crystals.

All About Fossils

Seashells are common types of fossils. These ammonites lived in the oceans around 100 million years ago.

Sedimentary rocks often contain fossils. As the sediment turned to rock millions of years ago so, too, did the bodies of plants or animals buried between the layers. Fossils show scientists life-forms that lived on Earth long ago.

The leaves of ancient plants are pressed flat in rocks made from mud.

This fossil shows that ancient birds had tails like reptiles and claws on their wings.

Do I know you?

Frizzle Fact
The oldest fossils are of bacteria about 3.5 billion years old.

How fossils form
by Arnold

Any sign left by an ancient living thing counts as a fossil. It could be a footprint or a piece of poop! It is very rare for soft body parts to become fossils. They rot away too quickly. Normally it is the hard parts — shells or bones — that are preserved. After being buried in mud or sand for many thousands of years, the body's chemicals gradually get replaced with rocky minerals. The result is a piece of rock in the shape of the original animal or plant — a fossil.

That makes an impression!

Fossil experts are called paleontologists.

This line of rocks was once the backbone of an ancient whale.

21

Mining

The world's biggest digging machines work in mines.

This is an open-pit coal mine. We burn coal as a fuel. Coal is a rock made from the remains of ancient forests.

Humans have found many ways to use rocks and minerals. For example, the metals we use to make everything from spaceships to spoons are locked up in minerals called ores. These useful rocks are often buried underground. Miners must find them by tunneling down to get them or by **digging** them out of huge holes called quarries.

Some real gems!

Precious stones
by Keesha

Precious stones or gems are among the various materials that are mined from Earth. Gems are shiny minerals with bright colors used in jewelry. The crystals are hard, which means that they are not easily scratched or cut. Diamonds are the hardest gems, so jewelers use saws coated in diamond fragments to cut crystals into shapes that sparkle. The four most popular gems are diamonds, emeralds, rubies, and sapphires.

Iron
Iron can come from hematite, pictured here. The ore has to be crushed and smelted to make pure iron.

Copper
Humans have been mining copper for 7,000 years.

Gold
Gold can be found as a pure metal or refined from an ore, such as chalcocite.

Frizzle Fact

The TauTona gold mine in South Africa is 2.4 miles (3.8 kilometers) belowground. Its tunnels are 500 miles (800 kilometers) long.

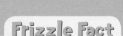

Inside a Cave

Earth's surface is not completely solid. The rocks that make the crust are riddled with caves. Most caves form when underground rivers dissolve soft limestone, creating amazing hidden spaces. Unusual rock formations develop in caves, like this one in Australia. They form from chemicals left behind by the water.

Cave pearls form in damp caves, where minerals coat grains of sand. Many coats build up over a long time, creating smooth balls.

Stalactites
These rocky spikes hang down like icicles. They form from minerals left behind as water drips from the roof.

Stalagmites
These pillars rise from the cave floor. They form from minerals in the water that drips from stalactites.

Frizzle Fact

Mammoth Cave in Kentucky has 400 miles (640 kilometers) of tunnels. It's the world's longest cave system.

Inside a Volcano

At the end of the day we arrived at what the Friz said was a volcano. It was a mountain with a dip at the top, which is called a crater. "Let's watch some new rocks being made," said Ms. Frizzle. Suddenly, ash, steam, and lava came spurting out of the crater with a roar. "Oops, we're too close! Hop in the bus, and let's get back to school."

Sometimes a volcano sends out a huge and super-hot cloud of ash. When it falls, the surrounding area is buried in a thick layer of ash.

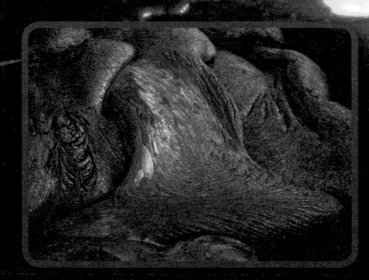

There are many kinds of lavas, but they all become solid as they cool.

Super hot
Lava is a thick liquid with a temperature of 2,000 to 1,500 degrees Fahrenheit (1100 to 800 degrees Celsius).

Volcanic fissure

Not all volcanoes are mountains. Some, like this one in Kalapana, Hawaii, are just openings in the ground.

Super-heated goo!

How do volcanoes form?
by Tim

A volcano forms where melted rock bursts out of the ground as an eruption. This can happen underwater as well as on land. Melted rock, called magma, forms below the Earth's surface. It is less dense than the surrounding rock, so it rises upward — like a hot-air balloon — through cracks in the Earth. Most magma solidifies before it ever reaches the surface, but in some cases it goes on to form a volcano. Magma that does reach the surface is called lava.

Frizzle Fact

The eruption of the Krakatoa volcano in Indonesia in 1883 was so loud that the bang was heard 3,000 miles (4,800 kilometers) away. That's the distance from Los Angeles to New York City.

Biggest, Greatest, Deepest!

Tallest sand dunes

There are giant sand dunes all over the world. A sand dune occurs where the wind blows sand into one enormous pile. This never-ending process can take several million years. The tallest sand dunes are in the Badain Jaran Desert in China. They are around 1,600 feet (490 meters) tall.

Largest river

Fed by streams in the Andes mountains, South America's Amazon River is not as long as the Nile River in Africa, but carries one-fifth of all the water in the world's rivers. It flows through the Amazon rain forest before reaching the Atlantic Ocean 4,000 miles (6,400 kilometers) away.

Biggest volcano

Hawaii's Big Island in the Pacific Ocean has two active volcanoes. Mauna Kea is the tallest, but Mauna Loa is the largest, and the biggest in the world. It has erupted every now and then for 700,000 years, and with every eruption it grows even larger.

Biggest Lake

The largest lake by volume in the world is Lake Baikal, in Russia. At around 25 million years old, it is also the world's oldest lake. It formed in a rift, where a crack is widening in Earth's crust. The lake is just over 1 mile (1.6 kilometers) deep. Around one-fifth of all the world's freshwater is in Lake Baikal.

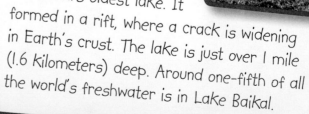

Highest waterfall

The waterfall with the highest drop is Angel Falls in Venezuela. The amount of water that flows over the edge is not very large, but it plunges for 2,648 feet (807 meters). That's like tipping a glass of water off the top of the world's tallest building, the Burj Khalifa in Dubai.

Tallest mountain

At 29,029 feet (8,848 meters) above sea level, Mount Everest is the world's tallest mountain. Mauna Kea in Hawaii is 13,803 feet (4,200 meters) above sea level. But, measured from its base deep under the sea, Mauna Kea is 33,100 feet (10,088 meters) tall.

Well done, class! I hope you can join me on our next adventure!

Largest cave

The largest single cavern is Son Doong cave, in Vietnam. Its name means "mountain river," and it contains an underground river and even a forest where sun shines in from an opening in the roof. The cave is 3 miles (5 kilometers) long and 600 feet (180 meters) high.

Driest desert

Although it is close to the Pacific Ocean, the Atacama Desert in Chile is the driest place on Earth. Around half an inch (1.25 centimeters) of rain falls here every year. That is an average for the whole desert — in some parts of the desert, it has never rained at all.

Rock Experts

The science that looks at the structure of planet Earth is called geology. Geologists study everything from how the oceans and continents have changed shape over millions of years to the way crystals form inside rocks. They have found that the planet is very old—it's been here for around 4.5 billion years.

❮ Geologist

A geologist tries to understand the history of the Earth by looking at the layers of rocks that can be seen at the surface. Rocks nearer the surface are newer than the ones lower down, and each type of rock was made in a particular way. Together the layers tell a long story about what the planet was like at different places and different times in the past. Geologists divide up the long history of the planet into a system called the Geological Timescale.

⌃ Geophysicists

Physics is the study of forces and energy. A geophysicist looks at the effects of such forces inside planet Earth. The heat energy coming from deep inside the planet makes swirling currents in the melted rock, or magma, beneath the surface. These currents push around the plates that make up the Earth's crust. As they move, the plates create earthquakes, volcanoes, faults, rifts, and mountains over the surface of the planet. Geophysicists also study the magnetism of Earth and the vibrations that run through the rocks deep underground.

Geochemist ❯

Chemistry is the science that looks at the way substances form and change from one type to another. A geochemist figures out the chemical processes that were involved when minerals formed to make rocks. Depending on the types of rocks formed, he or she can tell what the conditions were like on Earth at the time. It means that scientists can picture what planet Earth looked like a long time ago, when there was no one around to see it.

Words to Know

Altitude The height of something above sea level.

Ammonite An extinct sea creature that had a flat spiral shell.

Core The intensely hot, innermost part of planet Earth.

Crust The hard outer layer of planet Earth.

Crystal A clear, or nearly clear, mineral or rock with many flat faces, such as quartz.

Earthquake A sudden, violent shaking of the Earth, caused by rock masses rubbing against one another.

Erosion The process by which pieces of rock broken down by weathering are carried away by natural forces such as wind, water, or ice.

Fissure An opening or crack in the Earth's surface.

Magma Melted rock found beneath the Earth's surface. It is called lava when it flows out of volcanoes.

Ore A rock that contains a metal or valuable mineral, as in iron ore.

Sea level The average level of the ocean's surface, used as a starting point from which to measure the height or depth of a place.

Sediment Rock, sand, or dirt that has been carried to a place by water, wind, or a glacier. Layers of sediment become compressed over many millions of years to make sedimentary rock.

Sinkhole A hollow in an area of limestone that leads to an underground cavern or passage.

Smelt To melt ore so that the metal can be removed.

Swamp An area of wet, spongy ground: a marsh.

Waterfall Water from a stream or river that falls from a higher place to a lower place.

Weathering The process by which rocks change and are broken into smaller and smaller pieces by exposure to elements such as wind and rain.